C

<u>ERRATUM</u>

Page 29: Line 1 should read:
You are the tree strong as all storms would try

Page 62: Line 15 should read:
that under this concrete

IN HIS PAVILION
by MARION BUCHMAN

He shall hide me in His pavilion. PSALM 27:5

HASKELL HOUSE PUBLISHERS, LTD.
BROOKLYN, NEW YORK
1986

Published by Haskell House Publishers Ltd
Brooklyn, New York

Copyright © 1986 by
Marion Buchman

International Standard Book Number: 0-8383-2217-4
Library of Congress Catalogue Card Number: 86-080422

Printed and bound in the United States of America

ACKNOWLEDGMENTS

These poems have appeared in Arizona Quarterly, The Call, The Chicago Tribune, Crisis, Encore, Friday, Manifold, The Month, The New York Herald Tribune, The New York Times, Poet Lore, Poetry Review, Poet View, Redbook, South & West, Stanza, Sunday Times, Today's Poets, The Workshop Directory, The Writer, Writer's Digest, and others.

The poet's poems are anthologized in the following anthologies: Cheltenham Anthology of Prize Poems; Al di La Anthology of Prize Poems, Franklin College, Lugano, Switzerland; Answer From the West; Best Poems of the Twentieth Century; Diamond Anthology; Emily Dickinson, Letters from the World; Esoteric Anthol; Festival (Stroud, England Highly Commended List); First Annual Anthol. Of the New York Poetry Forum; From Sea to Sea (England); Great Poems of the Western World; National Federation of State Poetry Societies Anthol Vol 3; Parthenon; Peopled Parables; Poetry of Love, Past and Present; Poets of Today; Revue des Poetes Americains; Spring Anthology (Eng.); Stroud Festival Poems; Timeless Treasures (Gt. Br.); Tribute to Triumph; Women Poets Rising. Best Poets of the Twentieth Century.

POETRY AWARDS

Arizona State Poetry Society, Award of Merit; *Al Di La Prize, First Prize, Franklin College, Lugano, Switzerland;* Avalon Prize; *Cheltenham Prize, England;* Florida State Poetry Society, Certificate of Recognition; Idaho State College, Recognition; Indiana

State Federation of Poetry Clubs, First Place; International Writers Club Award; Ivan Franko Memorial Award, Distinguished Achievement Acclamation; John Masefield Prize, Eng.; Kentucky State Poetry Award; Kentucky State Poetry Society Certificate of Recognition; Kwill Klub Prize; Laudamus Te Award; Literature International Writers Club Award; Lousiana State University of New Orleans, Award of Honor; Magna Cum Laude form Manifold Magazine (England); Awards of Merit for poems, Manifold Magazine; Maryland State Poetry Society, Special Mention; Mentor Annual poetry competitions, many awards; National League of American Penwomen, numerous awards including those from the Matoon and from the San Diego branches; New Mexico State Poetry Society, Grand Prix Prize; New York Poetry Forum, Top ten List; New York Poetry Forum, First Prize, and First Place, several poems; Pennsylvania State Poetry Society, Grand Prix; Poet's Study Club of Terre Haute, Special Mention; Society of American Poets, First Prize, Bronze Medal Award; Stroud Festival Competition, Eng., Highly Commended List; Swinburne Prize, World Order of Narrative Poets; University of Southwestern Louisiana, Ninth Annual Writers' and Artists' Conference, won all five awards, 1969; Worldworks Contest, Prize; World Order of Narrative Poets, other awards; Writers' and Artists' Conference, Louisiana State University, First Prize; Writer's Digest Prize.

Memberships

The Poetry Society of America
The London Poetry Secretariat
Honorary Member, Maryland Council of English Teachers
Affiliate of National Council of Teachers of English

Poems taped, Library of Congress, 1977

POETRY READINGS

Notre Dame College
Rider College
Alice Loyd College
Essex Community College
Delta Kappa Gamma, Educators of Anne Arundal County
St. John's College
WBAL TV
WJZ TV
WITH
WEVD
Poetry Society of America
Poetry Society of Great Britain
New York Poetry Forum

POETRY WORKSHOPS

American University
Baltimore Free University of the Johns Hopkins University

INSTRUCTOR IN PROSODY

Baltimore Free University
Northwest Senior High School, Evenings at College level

Marion Buchman's poems, award certificates and other papers have been added to the Special Collections Department of the Johns Hopkins University Library.

TO VASILIS
and to my mother and father

CONTENTS

PART I

Some comments on A VOICE IN RAMAH
by Marion Buchman (Twayne)

ALLEN TATE
Marion Buchman is very gifted. Her book will create a stir.

ARCHIBALD MACLEISH
You keep a flame burning. Watch it well.

MARK VAN DOREN
The poems in "A Voice in Ramah," show remarkable powers of compression.

CARL SANDBURG
Marion Buchman's book reports to me that she lives in wide and wonderful arcs of sky and earth, and of mind and heart.

CONRAD AIKEN
How refreshing to find poetry that isn't afraid of having a sense of humor and fun! And that can go deep without pretence as in FIRSTBORN.

ROBERT HILLYER
A book of unusual poems whose general effect is impressive; that is to say, its aura, or whatever you choose to call it, clung to me sometime after closing the book . . . I thought the book had unusual power that shaped many memorable lines and phrases. It is very much alive.

RICHARD W.B. LEWIS
There is a distinct lyrical talent—a phrase I utter with much satisfaction but rather rarely. She frequently takes hold of an emotion, in fact of an experience in language that potently reacts upon itself—something like the successful short poems of Hart Crane, whom I was glad to see her celebrating.

OGDEN NASH
I read the poems of "A Voice in Ramah," with pleasure and admiration, finding in them great perceptiveness, tenderness and wit.

HOWARD NEMEROV
I am touched by the poems' simplicity and strength of their concern for children and childhood, something it seems poets have to remember just because the rest forget.

LIONEL WIGGAM
We have a great need of the feminine sensibility—the Adrienne Richs and Elizabeth Bishops are too few—and I earnestly hope Marion Buchman will keep producing poetry.

MORRIS BISHOP
I applaud her awareness, her aspiration, her achievement.

EARLE BIRNEY
I feel her delight in all peaceful things, forests, leaves, and loving hands—symbols very near to me.

NORMAN ROSTEN
I find the poems sincere, articulate, and lyrical in feeling—qualities which are increasingly rare in modern poetry.

MY MOTHER PEELING APPLES

I remember
the red spiral of peel
riding past her knife
its apple white flesh
dull as the peel was shiny
in an open May noon
when what bird sang
from our sidewalk's
cottonwood poplar
where my father
momentarily
snatched sabbatical?
Was it a cloudy
or a sunny
day?
I was as whole and joyous
as a juicy apple
the apple of my father's eye
in the eye of my bowing realm
whose suns
hailed me
whose stars
crowned me their apple queen

I remember the red spiral of years
riding past *time's* knife
the flesh of youth

A HAIKU

You broke the glass lake
Plunging, you made a flower
of churned green waters

GRAFITTI, U.S.A.

Names
uncarved
an anarchy

Names
that bleed their paints
and scatter seeds
of nomenclature

Derelict walls
sprout these gardens of
names
which flowers are cursive
with call

Missing is the amorous
M.B. LOVES V.H.

Names
separate   apart   alone
a jostle of solitudes
of alienations
that blossom
from the poison tree
of our century

O forests of names
what dove coos
amid your signatory blooms?

Names
that are onanism
where blow
cheated winds

Names
that litter strange seeds
in the fading States

FEATHER

White
  from an old red chair
Fright
  of some goose, broods there

Plume
  ruffle, flag of truce
Doom
  of some silken goose

GOUACHE

Airy
pale still life
dissolution
of form in light

tenuous existence on impastoed
ground of cobblestones

ah golden and shimmering
small and profound childhood
luminous island
of night purples and fog greens

rippling arches
vault that trembling air

Balloons of noons were druidic

There was a meticulous landscape
once visited
and already homesickness bloomed
where my first butterfly
sent me running in fear of its
unstudied wings

I now know they were flying petals
and that roses are pink wings

There is an invasion of past days
in my street
a fierce water color that dreams me

There were no ruffles but my dress
no tapestries except my soul's
ah sombre street

CHERRYWOOD HI-FI CABINET

Defoliated! cantata of blossoms
pink etude, May arpeggio of petals
a chorus of flowers (0 grained stasis)
Roots estranged shock the dark
where once giving waters slid away
Flight of branches careened, sun reeled
sky staggered

You are tooled to a box seasonless and walled
once airy temple

You fancy you are a winning seed
a root a shoot a tiniest tree growing growing
branching leaping budding leafing
you tower over rainy field.

A May morning you have become a great
pink cloud of flowers
an explosion of rosettes.

You dream to dower us
with globed red worlds of your fruit
and your exiled birds

CHOICE

Were I
A tall-stemmed rose
I should wish to live my life
not tossed
to a matador
nor clenched
in Carmen's teeth
not pressed
to sachet
nor distilled to a perfume
nor raised high
in the hand of a girl freedom fighter
but
I should wish
to be
in his favorite vase
on the desk
of poet Brodsky

NANCY HANKS LINCOLN

May sunlight brightened, hushed on her dark hair.
She hung the wash out and was unaware

she had conceived. Now, in this May, too soon
to know. Forsythia rinsed the glinting noon.

Nolin's Creek lay in new green innocence.
Birds flurried over. She leaned on the fence.

Dogwood posed proudly pink on sky and air.
She hummed a simple hymn, intoned a prayer.

A scraggly kitten mewed. She brought it milk;
called Sarah out to stroke its coat of silk.

Breezes blew sweetly in the wilderness
around the cabin's lonely dreariness.

Far off her heart heard drummers in a field.
An internecine war raged . . . . . . Peace bells pealed.

A great man spoke of "right" "malice toward none"
She could not know it was her unborn son.

May lengthened into June. She knew the rest:
Soon she would clasp a new child to her breast.

June golden as a molten vat of song
July and August, now the nights grow long

September and October cool with mist
crows barked and shrieked. The slanted sunlight kissed

the autumn fields with tenderness and light.
November and December blossomed white

beneath a holding snow through coming days
until a February dawn, when haze

of not too distant spring, hinted its charm
she lay with her new son upon her arm

on a rough wooden slat mattressed with husks
where winter rains came in through dawns and dusks.

Errands-to-do will come and griefs and joy
And you would see him lastly a young boy.

The youth behind the grocery counter, bore
your face and sadness. The young lawyer wore

your message to "Be good" "O nation, shine
My little boy lost me when he was nine"

Ruddy as a papaw the infant slept.
The days wore on. At last he grew. He crept.

He spoke. He ran. He laughed and played and cried.
When he was almost ten his mother died.

She died knowing he cared to read and write
on backs of shovels late in candlelight.

Growing as a tall tree, industrious, wise
she caught the look of mercy in his eyes.

Through all his trials and honors, hopes, despair
she was his lonely angel everywhere.

At Gettysburg she shared the soldier's plain
caressed his wearied brow and eased his pain.

And when he sat unknowing at the play
his mother dimly brushed a tear away

SUDDENLY ROADS DISAPPEAR

Here one white field where were streets
pleats every curb terrace-wise
lies to our wonder-struck gaze
glaze in a retrograde place.
Lace, opaque, mantles street names,
flames its pailettes wildly free
See now the snow is a page
rage of tree shadow, pink light.
Brightness is wilderness here.
Suddenly roads disappear

PIAZZA DI SPAGNA 26
(Keats-Shelley House, Rome)

The Via Condotti on that day
was sunlit. Persons went their way

along the piazza. I went in
past the stone boat square's trafficked din

into that hallway, up that stair
to your door, Keats! I entered there!

A paid guide lacking charm and graces
rolled back rose damask off glass cases.

Inside one (and each tied with care)
are two locks of your auburn hair.

I thought a moment of the sun
in Fleet Street; of Endymion.

In other cases, letters, notes
of yours and Shelley's; various quotes.

One Anna Angelotti's name
is linked but once here with your fame:

A rent receipt she signed to say
that you had paid your rent that day.

The famous drawing of your head
by Severn, with a note that read

I started this to keep awake
shows his devotion for your sake.

And now the room where Severn wept
(which fronts the plaza) where you slept

your final sleep. I look up to
the ceiling painted white and blue

its bright medallions scallopped, white
toward which you must have gazed at night.

Your bed is gone. Much here is changed,
removed and added, rearranged.

The life mask self conscious and kind
the death mask agony-confined

I gaze beyond the window, see
The Spanish Steps of Italy

in the rose day. Late morning thrives
with duller and less winging lives

TENANT

I neared my house
the residence I lease to others
as pensione

My tenant from upstairs
front rooms
was resting on the back porch
and gazing mistily
across The Spanish Steps

How pale!
So young
and dying
of the consumption!

His eyes dream.

I swear to you
as surely as I am Anna Angelotti
he will not outlive this February

His friend Severn
said "He coughs blood"

I hear he writes odes
to nightingales
—to autumn

IN THE ITALIAN ALPS

My pilgrim eye slowly explores the view
to the high altar of these Alps, the font
of pebble-bedded streams crumpling the sun
across the steepled pines.

Dark bridge. Tallow-like dripping waters run
straight down among the fretwork of the trees.
Another satin pliss'e river folds
its ribbon blue.

Stonefall of crenelated wall, proud birds
circle your waist. And the same shadows come
and go, as in dim centuries. You twist
the playful sun.

Here night is lost and nameless as the wind
when winter locks the gate by streetless stair
Anchorite of miled heights! Ai, Godcastle!
Holy carved flower of time!

CARDIOGRAM

Hurdy gurdy heart
riddling the world's street
with your song
metric measure of your innocence and grief
—of the once child
of the now grown child weary with sorrow
out on the blind air
alone alone alone alone alone
metronome
keeping time
against dissolution of the hour's force
whose past was poetry
and your correct father
whose hand
shaped your course of prayer

O chanting cardiogram
heart's penmanship
of stress and rest and stress
stanzaic scribble
of a life that suffered

turn, turn the crank of your music box
big
as my child-body

hail upon my day the stones of your anthem
breaking the light into crazed mirrors
—a Labrador seen from a jet
a composite soul with all travailed
dogs, cats, springs, summers, winters
where the seasons
mill through
the one   the lonely   the catching
the martial
heart

ZOO CAMEL

kneels
tent-like

His eyes dream Jacob
and Rachels

A wind rises
He sniffs burnoose
of breeze.

Unnoticed by him, a
caravan
of copper leaves
swept by
—October procession

There is a well in Ramah
and a misty hill there

His loneliness
is deep as that well
misty
as that hill.

Musty captive
in this shiny Egypt

CENOTAPH

Streets
of my history
joy buried under sprung clocks
and cracking calendars
where the narrative smothers

kingdom
whose lamplight
moons the cobblestones

homage
to you
streets
by flickering ghosts
of once-me
sketchy
in this full present.

All the rooms
dissolved into space
Now everything has vanished
not alone you, father
but even the scenes
of your youth

I am crushed by this empty site
by the weight of the nothingness here
once the definition of home.

Incunabula, O saga, form
shape, biography
who, in childhood's dominion
could have known your fragility!

O wanly lit
look at me.
In the wide urban renewal
of my snug phantom house
I am a pale icon.

What rash painter
painted out
the solemn dark red
of my street's houses and pavements
—my maroon Baltimore
whisked off the map
like a stage set?

O sacred statement of street
you ended like a torn crayon drawing
my massacred mandate, my lost law
childhood's kingdom
where

my father reigns now
in the candlepower of the past.

I stand
at a vanquished doorway
Father, take my phantom hand.

Somewhere here
shadowy
flickers your tenacious sabbath

ANCHORITE

Shut from blaze
of sun days
of snow craze

from bird ode
from scratched road
fast or slowed

barred indoors
safe from scores
public stores

I retreat
to this sweet
cell from street

dream apart
search my heart
ply my art

EMERGENCY

It happened
accidentally.
I was doing something else
when my finger flicked the universe.
I heard the world split
I looked
The globe lay unhinged
only gold space
like a
great and gilded dying mouth.
It was like a reverse suicide:
I did not quit the world
It exiled *me*

It occurred in a half second.
Intent on whatever else
I cracked open the world
The rift
was tinny
I saw the center
a vast gold silent outcry.

I had been neutral
indifferent
should have known it was there
should have taken sides
—a commitment.
That grand blue ball
with its encrustment of countries!
opal England, white Canada
mosaic United States

O I tried to close the cut
but jumbled the continents

LONGSHOT

Life is a casino
  where we play to win
    but we mostly lose

Life is a casino
  The roulette wheels spin
    where we chance to choose

Life is a casino
  where the cards are dealt
    and fate holds your hand

Life is a casino
  Dice tumble on felt
    Little ends as planned

THE FIND
News Item:

From the fifth millenium are found pieces of gold jewelry from an
Eastern Mediterranean royal tomb.

> Did she die old?
> Young?
> Her dust is antiquity.
> Yet this bracelet shines
> as when she showed it
> round her royal wrist.
> It speaks her touch, song, bread
> joys, tears.
>
> Wearing it
> she paraded
> far from the stranger death.
> This trinket
> commemorates her vanished name.
>
> Within its golden fence
> she descends a facing staircase
> her veils flowing blue clouds about her.
> Her fingers
> stroke a silk rope balustrade.
>
> She is lost past the stairwell of death
> her veiling a nimbus shift
> her bracelet a bright cipher

MARTYR TREE

The bough lifts me to meditation
teaches me its mantras
where the pond
opens its eye
where dawn wakens the waters

The tree
that only stands and waits
("They also serve")
awaits leaf
bud
flower

the tree
that dreads
but cannot
stay the placard
and
the
axe

YOU
For V.H.

You are the tree strong as all storms would *try*
Twined tightly round you love, the ivy, I

ASUNDER

From across the shroud of ocean
your absence is a death
you there, bearing flowers
the bouquet you never gave to me
that round word of romance

But what I miss and have now
is the sweet hollyhock of youth
you ever proffered
and the wry song of your laughter
these
among the brasses of the band
playing, red and gold braided
by the windy Thames
and these
from far and too long ago
I keep

and these
the flowers you did not give
that do not therefore wither,
the round word of romance
and now the ocean between
—that world of water
the watery land
that will outweep my tears.

ISADORA TO ESSENIN

My love is
the transparant green ballerina
whose lap
holds the ashes of your absence
that lustrous dancer
greyed with yesterdays

Her legs cross
at trim ankles
going nowhere

She is the shining nidus
that says
sensitive fires once flared here

My love is
that greygreen shrine

CITY SQUIRREL

Your ancestors
ranged the unnamed continent
whose natives
knew you
purely
Hiawatha's Adjidaumo.

Cavorting here
you conjure tents
and the lunar floodlight
by spirit trees

PASSIONFLOWER
(PASSIFLORA)

Circle
purple fringed above orchid sepals
Up from center a cluster of gavels

A crown
a twilit sun
a medal struck from earth
a dancer's outflared skirt
a purple language of fragrane
honeyed carpet of the bumblebee

A silent scallopped bell, its clapper poised
the bell, turned backward

a seed-sprung parasol

On ground lie the *fallen* flowers
like wilted closed umbrellas
while the vine twines
lit spiral lassos
on iron railing, porch swing
crabapple tree
Trefoil leaf
proudly lifts for light
ruffling in the wind.
Held tendril's spirals clasp.
Life ringed and crowned
by glory chimed of earth.
Courage opens its lavendar pavilion
against the snapped-closed parasol hour

Ray, crown, skirt, clapper, tendril
roof and bed
fragrance to wind's lesson of death
and seed in its season returning
memory, grief

THE DEATH OF MARTIN LUTHER KING

Who killed Martin Luther King?
"I," said the hater,
"As my nation's traitor,
I killed Martin Luther King."

Who saw him die?
"I," said the room,
"In a twilight gloom,
I saw him die."

Who caught his blood?
"I," said the world,
"In his flag unfurled
I caught his blood."

Who made his shroud?
"I," said the breeze,
"With petals from trees
I made his shroud."

Who'll be the clerk?
"I," said the lost,
"My plight was his cost.
I'll be the clerk."

Who'll dig his grave?
"I," said the flayed.
"With my little spade
I'll dig his grave."

Who'll be the parson?
"I," said the shaken,
"With a passage taken,
I'll be the parson."

Who'll sing a psalm?
"I," said the thrush.
"In this April's bush
I'll sing a psalm."

Who'll be chief mourner?
"I," said the dove.
"I mourn for my love.
I'll be chief mourner."

Who'll toll the bell?
"I," said Fame,
"Proclaiming his name,
I'll toll the bell."

All the doves of the world
fell sobbing and sighing
when they heard the bell toll
for Martin King's dying

COUNTRY OF NOW

In the alien country
of *now*
I miss the land
of *once*
grieve for the landmark:
My father.

Of his generous gifts
a misty little group
of red table and chairs
dreams
in a razed house

I could now only guess
the Eden
where
stood
home

CARUSO RECORD DURING A SNOWFALL

To wind's applause and confetti of snow
vignetted red velvet curtain opens.
The wide forest harp is silent past this window.
The poetry of your voice is cantata.

To veils of ovation and petals
of programs flickering beyond this glass
snowfall of gala days, white rosebuds
drifting, fell
—an arboring flood.

Fan letters, date pages avalanche
to the year's fastnesses, snow
of forgetfulness descending.

The aria of your fame, lentemente, maestoso
is dreaming in dark arcaded theatres.
The storm strums pizzicato on the white trees.

In my room now
in the theathre-in-the-round of the black recording
sleeps your voice.

The crystal lyre of landscape waits, awed
past my casement.

Your samite song is hosanna
to wind's applause
confetti of this snow

FROM A PILE OF OLD LOVE LETTERS

"Harry says you are very beautiful.
I would like to meet you sometime."

Now
yellow years later
O white words
Whose?

O unanswered
who were you?
Where are you now?

Your brave hope
dreams
in the dungeon of a drawer

CAPSIZED

The bridge
of my hope
sleeps
under the floodtide
of fear
by that house (drowned)
of love
the trees in an Atlantis
of amazement

The little sailboats
of frivolity
float
downside up
trailing their dragging sails
like fishing nets

THE ANAPHORA
(A LOVE LETTER)

O my dearest
How I love you!   O my dearest
How I love you!   O my dearest
How I love you!   O my dearest
How I love you!   O my dearest
How I love you!   O my dearest
How I love you!   O my dearest
How I love you!   O my dearest
How I love you!   O my dearest
How I love you!   O my dearest
How I love you!   O my dearest
these my tears   ↑ with you afar

HIS GIFTS

See how God
packages His gifts
Onions in gold foil
nuts in curved wood cases
garlic in purple and silver
and all seeds in fancy wrap
some with wings
And our durable frame
in precious flesh

See how He
protects these gifts
inner flesh of mollusks
with bright and shaped shell
inner bone of animal
cushioned

Utility and art
unite
in His great genius

MY JEWISH MOTHER

She came up betwen the waters
of Judah and of jazz.
Above the syncopation of the blues
King David's harp trembled
in her blood.

She came up dreamful
through the irrevocable corridor
where the non-unison singing
and the field hollers
flowed with trumpets of Solomon
into ragtime, jellyroll
and the march into Canaan

She was gorgeous. She might
have been joyful. But the hexameters
of the prophets
had drummed her blood blue.

Comely as Queen Esther
she walked with poetry
through alien plains
of prose
her feet sandalled
for ceremonial dances

DAY OF EMILY DICKINSON'S FUNERAL

Mr. Higginson came.
It was May.
A sunny day.
Marigolds illumed the lawn.

Inside the house
a glass of water embraced
violets.
On the piano
another tumbler of flowers.

Mr. Higginson looked into the box.
He regarded her domed brow.
"She is fifty-six
but looks thirty"
he thought.

Her sister
had placed two yellow flowers
into her hands
to greet G-d with

THE RIDERLESS HORSE

balked
was dragged
through the funeral.
Free, he might have soared
wild
past Pennsylvania Avenue
an emancipated Pegasus.

In Constitution Avenue he might have paused
—reared
(his body, closed as grief)
whose eyes glimmer their candle flowers
shade of those November leaves.

Hands harnessed his esprit
They did not hear the drum-roll of his heart

A pepole
saluted
their hail-and-felled

Through the white marble capitol
drifts
a riderless black horse

INSPIRATION

A pink
velvet
mood
envelops me
lounging
in G-d's mouth

Fierce rose
I rouse
on your
tongue

SNAPSHOT OF JOHN IN LONDON

Come
while there is sunlight
Let the impersonal camera
catch you on a day
and English day
the sun
spilled on your poetry hair
the sun
slant across your strong cheek
and chin
the sun
lighting the deep vers libre
of your eye
the light
on your Medici nose
slightly broken
as my heart
till you appear

THOUGHTS ON THE PAINTING OF A BRIDGE

Pastel music stirs
  in rose tones and blues
    and waves beyond a town
      beneath the bridge's throat

All his heart is hers
  that here gently woos
    from the held sunlight down
      to where cloud shadows float

Palette conscience blurs
  under storm of hues
    where sublimate they drown
      in the chromatic moat

NEHRU'S ROSE
(The One he Always Wore)

Wine dark and fainting
yet again reliving fragrance
like your sisters
for him
you kept inviolate
in silken sari
the secret of his proud and lonely heart.

His face and hands
were dreaming,
dusky flower

Inamorata
blessed, you wore his pulse
its votive drum
constant
on your frail cheek

DYING EARTHWORM

Raw
opalescent
a living wineflask
drying to a black slate
this
flesh

I throw it to the grasses
anonymous and suffering

O tiny wriggler
memento mori
emblem of the big sleep

VASILIS

My star! Event! I wait your return
from the fragrant isle
you so afar now
urging me back
my need, my mystic wine

Again you will wake to take me
in those long and measured stanzas of desire

At my white nightdress your hyacinth
is proffered, that fierce avowal!

Chance gave me you
a wash of wonder shining me to newness.
Through pink portals
of my tight secret
you break me into woman.
Our unconceived babes whimper
in my blood
with the King Tut treasures
of your endearments.

We are an ocean apart now whose waters
cannot drown love.

I recite your being
with my every breath.
My pulses race
with the amphibrach
of your name

FOR SALE

Two folding chairs
one table
one folding civilization

CHIEF CRAZY HORSE SPEAKS FROM HIS GRAVE

I see my world fragmented
like the tents of the Sioux
by the pale brother
see it lost
like the preliterate songs
of the Shoshone
under the same sun
that shone for those braves
and their forest
the once
great wooded land
I see that land rubbled
rubbed out
the plain trees, vanished
and I ask why!
Why?

The Great Spirit of the Dacotah
hovers over the stolen waters
And the fired sun none can steal
looks down his red eye.

Over the haggle of the bulldozers
I hear the ghosted buffalo feet.
In the stripped light
of my America's tree-poor morning
the soul of a nameless eagle lifts
He remembers the pure waters
the innocent buffalo
the naive tents
of the Sioux

HER WHITE DRESS
(After year 1855 Emily Dickinson wore only white.)

Mock bride?
Nun?
Priestess?
Dress, canvas for your miraculous paints?
O white moth.
Flower.

Was it anonymity's raimant?
Immortality's?
some dazzling doom
O vestal?

Was it a flag of truce?
A monument?
Your shroud?

THE CARDINAL

A scarlet flutter
and a quick utter
  of jewelled song
surprised and frighted
when I alighted
  he feared some wrong

Deep in the hedges
swift off high ledges
  he stalls for time
then hops up higher
that magic flyer.
  There is no rime

strophe nor metre
no poetry sweeter
  than what he gives
of tender chatter
and worlds that matter
  because he lives

REMINISCENCE

Nostalgia is a long distance runner
of lonely routes
whose heart's compass points memoryward
Ah what are those mythic islands
once real!
I voyage into that past
east to north to west to south to east
in a land overlain with the garnets
of homing
with the jade of strangeness
of pain

Dream bells usher me home
incense and candlelight
The faded and frayed faces
are retouched to newness
I call out silent
in a street of strangers

AILANTHUS

Ailanthus, tree of heaven, tree of the gods
misnamed "weed"
grows anywhere
in discouraging conditions
through cement
through sewers
in alleys
from window sills
on dump heaps
downtown
in slums

Indeed a tree of heaven
sprung up
in an otherwise treeless street
offering its gift of shade,
summers
its bounty of cool shadow
its fountain of leaves.
It seems a giant fern.
Winters, it is a stick

O my generation
Ailanthus "weed"
tree of heaven, tree of the gods.
Our world's tame wild great woodland
was long erased when you arrived
into this man-made desert. An arid nidus greeted you

Ailanthus, you reach toward light
your seed deep, darkly secret
Suddenly
—Tree!
The singing wings of hope

fly to your summering arms
Great promise of dawn
misty, cool, hushed
tremulous
a hanging pearl.
We squander you.
Prodigal idling stalls your word
O shade   O pearl   O shadow
of a great stock in a dreary land

Why does man pull all gifts downward?
Why is he destroying the world?
Is it that he dies
is finite
that he strips nature to death?
The hunter stalks peace and beauty
Ailanthus, poisons and fires surround you
Ah too beautiful! Threatened!

Serendipity
great flower
rooted in sand
skyward.
I bask in your structured wildness
your ordered whim
—a tree a child might scrawl
you have thrust out your lines of leaves.

Miracle, you are simplistic
as a primer
your leaved branches
lattices against the sun
—a net for the sun.

Ailanthus
you suffer the termite bulldozers

their sudden no-man's-land
once a forest

Ailanthus O wan hope
you stand
alone
your lyre falls
Everything falls. It is the law

Ailanthus, the wreckers
are chopping you
down
ending your pools of shade
Sun boils into the instant desert
O tree of heaven
tree of the gods
Glade falls to trade

Tree
laid low
horizontal
sudden bridge
to nowhere
your leaves fainting
in May's breath

You are born on rejectamenta
The city roars in.
Round the petals the emptiness

By the wharves
the chimneys
the steep roofs
the dormer garret window
mourns in my memory

Ailanthus, great green feather
anchored flashing wing

the soul breakers are here
We are dismembered in cracked mirrors
hill
grasses

Peace is your fiction
ideational, idyllic, ideal.
Nova. Star suddenly brilliant
suddenly dead
exploding star
falling star, life!

Ailanthus, ubiquitous, are you one root!
you spring up everywhere.
I saw you yesterday in the wan street
in the faded neighborhood.
I saw you lift through pavement
I saw you peeping round corner walls
I saw you living among the dead
I witnessed your lonely awning of leaves
O I have marvelled
at your grand hosannas
amid the lost dreams
lives, houses, ruins, the desert lots
where
blight carves incursions
smudges the bright page
of the street I read
literally
figuratively
interlineally.

I read sorrow   sorrow   sorrow   sorrow   sorrow
Sorrow, your winds are everywhere
And the short and the long *O* in your name
broods with the assonance
of a vast Ulalume

Ailanthus, a landscape splinters
like popsickle sticks
like the tiny strokes
meant as people
in Goya's *Scene of Toleda*

O hard-edge city
O stark colors
brasses of neon
the human, the animal
that startles

Skyward dancer
ascending rain
O continuum
are you one tree of one cavernous root
whose plants zoom up
here
there
legion!

Inamorata
The new cities rip you out
You re-seed yourself
You spring forth anew

In the old city
—its chips of sky
you wave a fan
You transcend polemics
Solitude invades your quiet blood

O my gutted city
you are sadder
than the ruins of Leptis Magna
Tripolitania
the Caracalla Baths.

I yearn for your wholeness forever lost;
presence of desolation
under ribbons of rain.

Ailanthus, sunward spray
how pure, how inviolate the world
while man sleeps

Ailanthus, you are song and text
incunabulum of the unending past.
I dream you are a remote star
an other world eye.

The moon lights candles in your foliage.
You watch the world torn as a web
where the bulldozers
are digging
America's grave
there where a waterfall
was rippling its silk.

For Sale on those trees
should read *Doomed*

Ailanthus, your hair
your wry smile
though foes conspire against you.

You mourn the roof trapped doves
of Baltimore
weed of grandeur, O tree
you riot everywhere

Dawn
window draperies are breathing
sinking, ballooning, sinking
ballooning, ballooning

ballooning, breeze-breathing
mockingbird jewelling the grey dawn
—gold thread through a pewter day

Conservation is a flower
predicatably threatened
It will be found crumpled
at the builder's chisel

Tree, you are deistic
at a deserted door
in the gateless places
the long lonely abandoned streets

Last of heroes
waving in a grassless avenue
believe
that under this concrete
a brook sings
under this pavement a path winds

Tree of heaven, O holy and profaned
where, the pilgrimages
in your honor
keeper of emptiness?
O desolate
O majesty
dishonored
What, your dreams
in the brooding winds?

You are a canopy over a necropolis
The posters of your palms
plead toward the untenanted
O inhabitor of the uninhabited
habitu'e of solitudes

You speak the dying nation
its scarred streets
its fractured fronts
its epidemic of hollowness

My city, terra incognita
We have hung our harps upon the willows
How shall we sing a song
in a strange land
our land

In a fanfare of folly
there are celebrations
but far, ailanthus
far from your environs

Fireworks flare
showers of pink and green explosions
which you might glimpse
in the high far circle from you

You are
a psalm
a poem
ancient
new

You sign your roots
in the mysterious dark
your stanzas in that dry deep
you stand to a last center
open as a syllable
a lisp
where loneliness is is total

Teacher, someone loves you
Somewhere

in the silent night someone cares
that you say your staves
to a void
Someone cares that you consecrate
the vacant days
the awesome nights.
Speak
speak
O heart and visionary.

Your course is downward
upward
outward
root
branch
Speak newly, bough
somehow a survival.

Will that day come when

They shall not hurt nor destroy in all my holy mountain
Brother shall not lift up hand against brother
Neither shall they learn war anymore
The lion shall lie down with the lamb
And a little child shall lead them
And the earth shall be covered with the glory of G-d
As the waters cover the sea

O my country
stricken with pollution
your tree is trying
its blossoms appear
where no spring flows
its branch heavenward
groping
its hands

64

pleading *hosanna*
hebrew
for *O save us*
O save us   O save us   hosanna   hosanna

Timeless
you are our symbol
of the dream unactualized
of the hope that prospers.

Afar
trumpets of petunias
blare pink
a handless clock lisps foolishly
tells no time
promises no future
dreams no tomorrow

There are bracelets
to break your wrists
necklaces to throttle you
Far from you bedlam crowns a vapid glory
Sic transit gloria, sic transit gloria
sic   sic   sic   sic   sick

Ailanthus, you overcome the drought
You have survived a world
of blade and flame
Will you be our last prophet?
Come, I shall sit under your store of fans
I shall regard you
you, the unnoticed
I shall ponder the book of your leaves
I shall hail, I shall hail
your interlinear sky

Ailanthus
door to space
door to no one
door to the tomb of a nation.
Where, the bearers of roses?
Why is our newness frayed as Pompeii?
abandoned?
A throng of papers festers at your feet
O holiest rubble in a dust
of all yesterdays
O devout and maligned
O swept empire of once

Ailanthus, you are a cenotaph
A band plays a silent music
a grandstand vanished as a petal
gleams in snuffed light
It is the night of the nation
the night of the soul

Beginning, end, beginning, end
supple, airy
you will remain
a last coat of arms
O ensign
your flooding hair
its lake of shade
I beheld you yesterday
We saluted each other

You are trained to a city
a tunnel sky
You wake
sad
into a world that man is unmaking
You blossom in a wasteland
its losses drain your blood
You would return to sleep

to escape the shock
of waking.
The destroyer is loose
in our holy mountain
bringing it down
sahara-ing the rose

The clock cracks the calendar
We sense our momently losses
The falling off of our pristine heritage
settles in our bones
We are washed in pollution
We are washed up
washed away.
Only the stain
we have made of our world
remains

Good-morning, bad morning of the midus hand
Good-morning, mourning, mourning
Dawn silence stirs
with clank of day
Cat
dog
all the homeless
are our charge
their hunger, thirst, dangers
their vulnerable hides

We don earrings and bracelets
cravat and hat
in burning Babylon
We are at a tower in Shinar
All is a jargon of gibberish

O we know that we will go down in history

history
history

O we know that we will go down in
in
in

O we know that we will go down
down
down

O we know that we will go
go
go

O we know that we will
will
will

O we know that we
we
we

O we know that
that
that

O we know
know
know

O we
we
we

O
O
O

Save us this morning
morning myopic with strontium
in the razed woodland
in the kingdom of overkill

Ailanthus, moon nacre
pearls your night palace
glittering you lonely

Sometimes in the lost night
you become a rain castle
in a glazed moat
Today you are ensign
O sentinel
I touched your tender leaf
I salute your exotic flags
I review your troops
O trees

In the embrace of your canopy
I know your vatic voice
your fey dance
in twilight's pink pavilion.

Ailanthus, I am a pale flower
on pilgrimage here
in your august presence.
You receive me
in your summer raimant of
pink and green

One winter you welcomed me
You were leafless
golden in your nakedness
as a nocturnal sun.

On the Fallsway
I saw you bowing in the winds of dusk

And by doorways long abandoned
you call from the mildewed wall.
Dusk.
I weep for the unvisited veins of your leaf.
Wherever you gaze
you live on the edges of grief
like joy.

Where the signs bleed and falter
(their broken wings)
—where wait the dying houses
the unbreathing chimney
—where the garret window stares stone blind
how empty
the echoey rooms
of your world
O new failing Samaria!

Where we see city
should be field
where we see blight
should be splendor
where we see slum
should be woodland
where we see fraud
should be love

America
your dead stores
your perishing streets
I could not dream your husks so sad
A Herculaneum
almost a catacomb

Ah pariah tree
among the rubbish and the transients

anchored
arbored in ashes.

On your dais of rubble
none hears your cavatina
inamorata
inamorata!

I have traced the republic of your pulse
Treasury
who has counted these leaves
these books of your body
O friendly and misnamed?

Breezes hear your Modeh Ani
at daybreak
your nightly Kriah Shema

Ailanthus, no lover woos you
nor regards your waking
silhouette outcast
loverless
lost.
Strangers move past your gutted gates
out of time.
You have outlived the broken pinions
of shutters
the leveled house
You yearn for the vernal
summers stripped away
the paths
whose pale petunia trumpets ripple
and fade
yet you gather the world's morning
you wager peace
you wait with your gifts and history

71

But no one comes
I will come
for I have regarded you
I shall come
I shall thank you, glowing, humble
for my prize.

You shape the landscape
to a templed garden
among our flat roofs.
In the American silences
you wait for us
in the swift dawns, the long nights.

And now you seem a nightwatchman
in a fortress
trying a new poetry
where the factions
refuse to coalesce
and instead
are exocentric as a fountain
the fountain upward that falls

Everything falls
It is the law.

Anachronism, you throw a tree shadow.
Ailanthus. World dropout.
Posterity knocks.
In a dry century
out of a prayer book page I hear Amos:

Remove from me the noise of your songs
And the melody of your viols I refuse to hear
But let justice well up as the waters
And righteousness like a mighty stream

ODE TO MY FATHER
In Memoriam

Goodbye, all lonelinesses here convene
fenced round me sure. I am their heiress, lost
who seeks explicit meanings, am betrayed
by innocence whose flower to me is tossed

that withers in my hand. Goodbye, I weep
unknowing, unresigned, found under sky
needing your warming hand, the majesty
and splendid hue of your caressing eye.

Suddenly I am here a child again
caught in a poem of sadness wanting praise.
The pyrrhic minutes will predictably
run ever through our caesura of days.

Spondaic time where farewells will return
penultimately sighed, I wait in vain
his dear phylacteries of faith to know.
Earth's talisman of love wakes not again.

Goodbye, goodbye, my heart is desolate
where leaf by leaf the roses fall and scrape
the roadless ground of hope with their dry signs
that pile to heap interstice of escape.

Marion Buchman

PART II

From "A Voice in Ramah"

The Early Poems

TABLE OF CONTENTS

THUMBSUCKER

Fear flies to the womb
grief, to the tomb
bride takes the groom.

FIRSTBORN

I saw no infant
but rather, the frightened never-understood
young girl
the matron who hated old age
and then the old woman
embroidering life with memory's heavy thread
I heard no child cry
but storms rage
I saw time erode even the last inscription
on her stone
and so I wept
when they brought her in.

PRELITERATE CHILD

Behold, the pages of a book
are streets, horizonless and bright
gateways through whose interstices
stares an all still and snowy light

the rolling lines of sentences
are fences black on a white sky
the square light of this page is cold
as window where blown snowdrifts lie

Turn, turn the lost enchanted child
to picture page happy to see
whose blues and overwhelming pinks
will harbor and a garden be.

KINDERGARTEN SUBSTITUTE TEACHER

Her face is wordless, naked as a page
where story is unknown and beckoning
is innocent as any open moon
full on a foreign landscape new as frost

What waits behind the crisp and shining cover
whose leaves preliterate hands are warm to try?
They feel for her whose little faces gleam
like satellites 'round a discovered ball.

There is a fixed air like a butterfly
clapped under glass for every pondering stare
Children are always lost and kind and searching
and substitute means "stepteacher" to them.

INFANT

Blind mouth that roots for breast like a moist bird
Innocent voice lost in a void of cold
Love not yet guile, nor tenderness yet word
return us to the ancient newest fold.

Oh flailing outflung arms in a distress
of wooshing air, of unembracing space.
Oh redness and the flower of the womb
Oh tiny oh devout and poet face

Oh fluttering fledgling, we shall long endure
with will toward peace, your tiny shining need
with cotton-soft emollients till the war
curve to a birth—its agony, love, creed.

FIRST SNOW

Winter's big book
opens
its
first
white
page.

SUMMER TREE

Green words
  in garret eye
  intensify
  syllables sigh
sea birds.

PAEAN TO CHILD

Child, your love's fingers twine about my hours
their innocent pink wonder at the world.
and tear my bitterness with their fierce flowers
until despair is crushed, in their cup curled

Dear child, your hands are flowering with fairy
over the fevered and world-weary face
of this lost plot—are calyx and corolla
that, somehow, hold a breaking world in place.

LEAF

A wet noon, the child at my hand, and the leaves,
I pick one, the largest, the russet, that grieves

I trace it on pliable clay and I mold,
I own it now glazed and ceramic and cold

It holds the green golden day when we walked
I and my child as we sang and we talked

It keeps the warm power of mind and of hand
that kneaded and glossed it to harbor, to stand

DIVA

A little child riding is singing
soft as her gold blowing hair
buttercup praise
a green story of grass

Life, love and time plaited together
into a long, yellow braid
tied at the end
with a ribbon of joy

SHARON'S EYES

Sky and forest sunlit wholly
summer noon sunlit and clear
leaves ashimmer, pools aglimmer
vernal equinox is here

GRANBY STREET

Life was mud pies and fireflies
dust and dazzle of childhood
sure and glorious

On that corner by the harbor
the pocked house stands this pale day
where the greay street sins and forgives

No water whispers past the pier
though ships rumor the bay

How small my street once seen wide
O treeless, here our green wonder blossomed
O grassless, what bright laughter rippled here

Dusk
sacred chimes splinter the time
into the sighing day

A missionary with no missive
walks woodenly between two wars
a wan child chants stanzas

I peer into my heart
and behold a place, strange, broken
bandaged with splints
and know my heart you are my vagrant house

PUPPY

All hail
his merry tail.

THE WHITE CAT

The white cat of joy plays with the string of circumstance
romance is a catnip whim
him it delights
Nights under a white-lanterened sky
high he springs on airy feet for a stone
lone his glee is company enough

The white cat of reflection is more proud
loud he purrs his glories and his peace
fleece of white reclining in the sun
one white sign like silence and a truce

The white cat has his frenzies and his fears
years though will never find him in despair
glare glorious is all his outrage wears
bares tooth and claw to tear a world apart
dart from his rage, his fear can climb a wall

The white cat of sleep is best of all
fall from all else his slumber is a realm

WAR LOSS

Here is where they found her
    sighing last "My child!"
flies and fires around her
    and a jet gone wild.

SCHISM

They rocket but I stumble
   into war
but I fumble
   at my door.

I whisper but they thunder
   at the gate
and I wonder
   at their hate

They shadow the tall grasses
   where a child
wounded passes
   to death's wild.

SARA ERICA

Her eyes are leaves that sparkle warm
around an amber light
and softer than a robin's breast
they whisper sun's delight

they are a gold more genuine
than gold of high renown
Daisy, sunflower, chrysanthemum
sing in these eyes of brown.

BERCEUSE

Baby
　dying
strangers
　crying

flies swarm
　closing
on his
　dozing

maggots
　feeding
on his
　bleeding

cannon
　shatters
God to
　tatters.

MINK

Frightened little furry paw
   captured in the trap
though you cry, you will die
   to make milady's cap.

Blood and snow and iron wind
   on a bitter trap
down you sink, little mink
   to be Miss Twaddle's wrap.

GHETTO

Dust over Warsaw is a hawk
that picks into the board and stone
and maze of children who were whipped
by armored men to die alone.

Hush over Poland hears the paean
broken to pity and surprise
into a monument where steel
lies quiet to their eyes

Dawn over Leszno Street rolls gauze
of light too late for these brave poor
whose courses paralleled and crossed
the purple, yellow plaid of war.

PLANE

When I hear a plane I shrink
in that dread that makes me think

of a jellied gasoline
poured like rain on a cold green

I can see the people run
from the terror of the gun

mothers ill with fright and ire
at the deadly napalm fire

Land of Morning Calm—the plane
and the broken children slain

FURLOUGH

I need threnody and darkness in this house
the light is anomaly
for I must feel my day
I must drink my fill of those grave eyes
in the shadow
see the shade cut
across the dear hollow of your cheek
and play its sweetest dirge there
Yours is a beautiful face
We will not speak
we will not let us weep
we will deliberately laugh
into each other's hearts
and it must be beautiful
for we know what we should say.
Dare not look as if you have just come
or as though you may leave
lie in this sombre room
like some hero
who cannot pass away
for you are the cannon's
more than ever mine
the colder arms know you
and I cannot bear to have you really
kiss me
though your eyes caress.
Remember when I said you
looked like Dante?
Before the drums
stay with me still
awhile

though our mouths touch not
nor our thighs
I have need
only of those tragic hands
the earnest clasp of them
and then
"Tout est perdu fors l'honneur."

CHOSON

Mommie, why does light look livid
  where gleams leaf and bird gold song
Baby, star shell bombs are vivid
  baby, voice of jets is strong

Mommie, why do steel birds thunder
  and make black parade in sky
Baby, you are young to wonder
  you are young to question why

Mommie, how the winds smell acid
  and the world cut at its breath
Baby, once our land was placid
  now the only rest is death

Mommie, why snatch me from household
  running, running in the roar
of machineguns in the dark cold
  Baby, dear one, this is war

Mommie, mommie, blood is racing
  from my head and down my eyes
yet you fall and leave me facing
  lead and fire from hills and skies

WAR REMNANT

Seven yerars old, he stands with all the others
   as maimed as he and orphaned and forlorn
learning so soon to question like his brothers
   "Was it for this a little child is born?"

dimly he can remember holding treasures
   like crayons, even trivial sticks and strings
now without hands he knows these as the pleasures
   of boys with hands who do so many things

Infancy and senility lock coldly
   to prison helplessness within his heart
he would avoid your gaze but never boldly
   Checking his tears he feels his eyelids smart

Of what use now a picture book to scrawl
or silver spoon or drum or bouncing ball?

TARGETS

No emblem emblazons their glory
no song anthems out their dark story
yet these are the children, the sorry.

No door opens welcoming token
and all the soul's windows are broken
Yet these are the gentle, soft-spoken.

In night and ice, star shells shower
guns spite, bombers riddle the hour
on these who are psalm-song and flower

YEAR 1AA

This is the hour
whether the primal flower
would bloom or break
over the pavement of propriety
and—oh it mattered not
at the close
where all the world
tore downward to its end
whether the lamp or breakfast bowl or bed
remained or shattered
whether the walls stood
or splintered
in that one mushroom of wild light and sound
man's craft and art dissolving

where would stand
the balanced warm tomorrow?
Only the lonely leaf seared briefly
the forsaken grass charred momentarily
the field flowers, shocked, remain
under the
pale rotunda of the sky

TOMB OF THE UNKNOWN SOLDIER

In the unwindowed house
the lovely and plundered, though sundered are one
now none is left who remembers the street that is gone
Easily, like dawn or dusk, he loved

Silence locks him past the pomp of music
Whiteness holds him past the flood of flowers

Over the curve of eye
the clay lid dreams eternity

REAL ESTATE

Once the night was a dark forest
   where a rock-strewn brooklet rang
now the trees are down and daylight
   cuts too sharply where birds sang

once the dawn was a hosanna
   draped about in green and rose
who can tell me where the wonder
   of the magic woodland goes

STREET IN THE WOODS

There is a forest in the city.
There the crickets in their loud season are safe
from the marauding children whose lawless hands
are innocent.
The sleek crow streaks a blue-black rippled line
across a cut of sky and swath of woods.
One day a red bird lit on a bare branch—
a momentary plump and crimson bud.
There is this god of green in spring
that rings my block of street—
street at day a strict rectangle
a sunken sun-drenched harbor in a wild
at night a necklace gemmed with yellow lights
laid down upon black-velvet wilderness.
This is the forest in the city
the city in the field
Unseen by man the brook tinsels and glows
over stones
the white brook rolls and purrs
and here the child sings its white hurrah
its banner soaring
scrawled importantly.

GLOBE LOCUST

Lollipop on a stick
a slender girl with green hair
a ballerina
inspired by the wind
a stranded gypsy.

ESCAPE

Here the avenue parochial
the tense hedge the strict street
with brag of facade
only the alley ashamed and democratic
my heart is not here

but there
where no ground rent or proud fence can be
nor slighted flower blossom

there my heart is
gathered to the salt breath
where that flurry of birds
whose lasting snow whirling
lulling with their feathered bells
the gulls spell love

DEFIANCE

I have seen melted wax but flame still burning
and sea moss torn yet floating on the sea
Seen the travail of men who still were yearning
for life though it held only agony

RUINS OF WARSAW

The guilt
of the beetle
is in the perforated leaf.

OCEANSIDE NIGHT

Her mantle dark about her
skirted with lace she glides
and sighs in that moonlight
under those stars
this I remember

Over the water-scalloped sand
hear the swish of glistening hem
this I desire
would leave hyacinth and vines
now
for where the gull sleeps

LIGHTNING

A silver branch
flashed through
the sky

drops crystal globes
of rain
like blossoms

ROSE

I sing the rose unpetalled like red drops
the leaf lost in November's yellow hand
twilight, the winter sea and ever love
its free, resurgent and gigantic land.

REBEKAH TO ISAAC

A reed
a flower
a shin-
ing hour

soft song
a blueness
etern-
al newness

embrace
and longing
and child-
ren thronging

a stream
a willow
and love's
green pillow

a thrust
of tower
a rush-
ing shower

heart, soul
and weather
all rolled
together

you are
and hold me
so shy
so boldly

DAVID PLAYS THE HARP

His fingers in that filmy drapery
  awaken music breaking to the swirl
and shimmer of the high meridian sea
    whose wind-swept hands of weather knit and purl

a scarf of pastel words like sunny flowers
  drifting across the windows of the sight.
His face behind that curtain of stringed hours
  shadowed, is glistening like candlelight

The summer wafts its honeysuckle song
  and eventide dips soft wing down like dove
night's dark blue tower strikes its silver gong
  his hands sing treasures and unfasten love

POET

I am the flame, my poetry its shadow
blow this fire and the dark disk moves, swims in wind
thinned to the substance one can touch but not hold
gold for its light that blesses and holds danger
stranger to waters whose salt is not sorrow
morrow in a tiny tongue hot as the sun.

ALONE

The night is a cold hearth
a last burnt match
sharp shadow and dark sound
and a sprung latch.

WOMAN

A candle, my desire dances
wind's wanton one, the wick's despair
in the stiff room would kindle worlds
but held in candelabrum bed

stands lost and bends, stands lost and melts
silently in the deepening dark
Beaded and draped my body flowing
coheres to form one lithic tear

THIS GYPSY PRINCESS

A song of rain
spun out of the dark blue
streamers ran into gilded
opals
and she came
a flower of a girl
half child half woman
dark hair like night
round her white sholders
framed a loveliest dream
those almondine eyes
were slant songs
green-praising spring
She glided to the gusty swell
a poet
ah princess
legend
tiara of rain in your hair
lone at your gypsied feet
the lipless trees.

JOY

Is a wing
that can sing

is a word
like a bird

chirps a trill
that will thrill

bowls of sky
downturned high

RETURN

The waves wash their green woe
What if tomorrow comes and comes again
like senseless foam. The sea is the sea
whether its bed or its ripple
Surface tells us as much as any glass
with memory of mirrors
yet that glass is kind holding no secret
more than remembrance
We pass and leave its face to light and walls.

Your dear hand presses kindly at the door
where she left you with heartbreak long ago
there are no tears but only things that warp
like face seen in a stream
or hair reflected in an ever-rippling pond
the hours run together like ringed waves
of grief struck into life by careless stones

DANCER

Darling, I dance for you
to the beat of victory cymbals
out of may chains like Cybele
I drift on stage gowned in red
like blood, in gold like sun
in flesh like liberty.

With the strings and the horns
and the trumpets swelling
I dance.
I dance bread, I dance the equal wine
I dance life
I dance battle, death, sorrow
birth, celebration, festival
endless, rapturous
shining in the dim hall
of our night
till dawn's pale lanterns bloom across
the east
to light us to an accolade
of love.

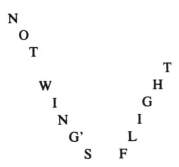

```
N
  O
   T
                 T
   W           H
  I           G
   N         I
  G'      L
   S     F
```

nor descending a stair
                        (step
                              by
                                meas-
                                    ured
my desire is   step)
              d
                o
                 w
                  n
                   h
                    i
                     l
                     l

all the way
down forever
down the endless steep .
walls crumble to it
tree trunk's roundness whisper
"Roll through, roll past"

my desire for you is a
rushing downward
under streaming moons
I am hurled
on and down
down
down
to closing sea

WAR GRAVE

There are children here who never knew their names
or love or laughter or small children's games
whose hours were threadbare, bleeding and afraid
They sleep for whom at last one bed was made.

IN THE QUARRY

As water, slid from heights, that will not rise
up to the known horizon, my despair
is lowest and is level on the deep
and comprehends only the towered wall

Your flowers of love and longing smother me
I answer with impatience though with pity
I want to scale the giant side of habit
several of whose stones give way before me

EPISODE

Now more than name the known eyes warm are voyage.
The taut venetian blind against that sunset
shut fast to dusk within the strange place, bore me
on orange-colored corrugating waters
out past the cloud of land and line of bridge
into a vortex. Turning new, swung high
toward peninsula Christ-tipped and huge
beyond my orifice of faith I start.

Be street a field locked in one late fleet Maytime
but only for the violet of your eyes
but only for the secret flowering warm
that was your hand's touch in the public square
sun-splashed and sad and sanctimonious.

I break. O chrism spilled on cicatrix
oh loved, rejected, come, return, return!

SOLSTICE

That rains this summer out is our dismay
Where bursting blossoms crack and disappear
the rosy-golden sky strikes into grey
the flowering green leaf suddenly turns sere

the winds that blow southwesterly sigh snow
seaward oh seaward over sunless sands
into the systole of undertow
cold as the arctic of our parting hands

ELIZABETH BARRETT TO ROBERT

As by its stir a wind
    As by its note a bird
As music with one reverie twined
    I guess you by a word.

Through dusks of shadowy space
    And time unstirred—unstirred
Until I know your hand, your face
    I guess you by a word.

SOJOURN IN MALLORCA

Scudding clouds muddy the morn
torn by the sudden dark.
Mark this violent twilight

At noon. Hard virtue prevails
fails only in our private room
gloom sacking sensuality.

Proud hunger soon must end
rend or resolve at last
fast—or must feast. How shall I wait:

Bloom burns and bruises, warms
alarms despair. Till blossom dries
sighs still betray me lusting, lost.

Honor is gossamer yet holds like rock
mock ignorance a ritual in our heads
beds will belie with lust known holiest
Best is the swelling wonder of our love.

THAIS

Clean as that desperate noon (her conscience waning)
blood's sun like seed flared whiter than his flesh
whose passion unto its last consonant
tore through her nuptial veil to pristine wonders
swept her like leaf into an avalanche

Hot as that hour now love's wall complaining
brands hard his name as memory breaks sleep's mesh
That instant burns planned and recalcitrant
while new and rude a giant rapture plunders
her guarded prison garden root to branch

CROW

Argument in a black wing
has no joy taught you how to sing
is there no sight you ever saw
could change into a song your caw?

THE UNINQUISITIVE

Never whatted
never whyed
grew up very
mystified